FOR THE GOLFER WHO HAS EVERYTHING

A Funny Golf Book

TEAM GOLFWELL

FOR THE GOLFER WHO HAS EVERYTHING, A Funny Golf Book,

Contents

Introduction

This unique golf book has everything with its funny, true and little-known golf tales, jokes, insane golf courses, hilarious quotes, world golf records, and much more in this entertaining and amusing book and can be shared with golfing friends, or on the 19th hole, or anytime!

This book makes an enjoyable and funny gift for the golfer, a great Holiday gift or stocking stuffer, as well as a gift for any occasion. Great to keep on the bedside table, read while traveling, or anytime! He'll love you for the laughs it brings!

As Arnold Palmer said many times, the game of golf requires "complete concentration and complete relaxation" and a good laugh will clear a golfer's mind, release tension, and make him relax and play golf better.

"Look at Lee Trevino. He's always laughing. It's hard to be tense when you're laughing. Laughter is the safest, nicest tension reliever I can prescribe."

- Dr. Rudolf Laveran, Psychiatrist, from "Why Golf Drives Us Crazy" by Jeff Silverman

Amazing Golf Courses and Special Golf Holes

World's longest golf course

The world's longest golf course is approximately One million four hundred ninety-two thousand and seven hundred and eight two (1,492,782) yards long. That is a little over 848 miles long.

The course is called Nullarbor Links and is an 18 hole par 72 course along the barren Eyre Highway in Western Australia. It takes four days to complete and runs from Kalgoorlie to Ceduna, in South Australia. There is one golf hole in towns over this over 800-mile stretch. It is presently closed due to the Covid pandemic.

The Nullarbor Links is unique. The 18-hole par 72 golf course has one hole in each participating town or roadhouse along the Eyre Highway from Kalgoorlie in Western Australia to Ceduna in South Australia. As you travel to the participating town, you'll find each hole includes a green and tee and rugged outback-style natural terrain fairway. Very Australian to say the least and a very popular activity/attraction along the renowned desolate Eyre Highway. [1]

According to the Guinness Book of World Records, the longest "normal" golf course in the world is the Jade Dragon Snow Mountain Golf Club in Lijiang, China which is "only" 8,548 yd (7,816 m) long. The longest hole is a 711-yard par 5 and the par for the course is 72. [2]

Largest Sand Trap in the World

The largest sand trap in the world is in Portugal at the new Krisirk Resort golf course. The huge trap was designed by Walther Mittë.

The bunker is called Nunca Sera and guards the 165m par-three 13th hole on the Pura Ficcao which is the first of two courses at the resort. It is 22 meters or 72 feet deep.

The trap is steep, and balls fall to the bottom of the trap. So, you must hit it at least 72 feet in the air to reach the upper lip of the bunker. [3]

Longest Par 3 in the World

The longest par 3 in the world is called the Extreme 19th that is 391 yards long and 400 meters high above the green (about 1,312 feet or 455 yards) and it takes approximately 30 seconds hang time before the ball drops to a green. The green is in the shape of the continent of Africa. You must take a helicopter up to the tee and this very unusual golf hole is at the Legend Golf resort in South Africa. [4]

Golf in the Nude

"Nice butt!" The La Jenny Resort in Aquitaine, France is according to their website, the "Only Naturist Golf Course in the world" featuring a 6 hole golf course where you can play nude and is a popular resort for Naturists. Also, according to their website, the resort has "a competent, qualified, available, passionate, and attentive team that offers internships, individual lessons, and individual coaching. Bring sunblock if you decide to play it and it sounds like a great bucket list course! [5]

Highest Golf Course in the World

Where on earth would the highest golf course be located? The Himalayas, of course. The Yak course is near Kupup in East Sikkim, India, and is an 18 hole golf course. It claims to be the highest in the world at 13,025 feet and is a par 72 being 6025 yards long. You must become acclimated to the altitude and greatly reduced oxygen to be comfortable and enjoy this course.

The course is generally playable from May to December subject to snow conditions. During the winter months, there is ice skating and skiing available.

Needless to say, it is recommended to have a yak to help move around the course. Try the Yak burgers at your own risk. [6]

Highest Golf Course in America

The Copper Creek Golf Club in Copper Mountain, Colorado is the highest course in the US being almost 10,000 feet (9862.20 ft.). Designed by Pete and Perry Dye, Copper Creek has amazing views of the 10 Mile Range. The front nine goes through alpine terrain, pine forests, lakes, and streams.

The back nine cuts through forests and remnants of a Nineteenth-Century mining town. Another bucket list course for the adventuresome golfer. [7]

Lowest Golf Course in the World

This course is listed in Golf Digest's "America's 50 Toughest Courses." The Furnace Creek (aptly named) is in Death Valley, 214 feet below sea level. It is the lowest altitude golf course in the world. Temperatures can reach up to 130 degrees.

This 18-hole par 70 course has Palm and Tamarisk trees on the sides of fairways with amazing mountains visible from all areas of the course.

The course was redesigned in 1997 and water penalty areas are on nine of the holes. It has also been designated as a "Certified Audubon Cooperative Sanctuary" by the Audubon Cooperative Sanctuary System (ACSS) of Audubon International. [8]

Death Valley is appropriately named, of course, as the extreme summer heat can cause death. In the winter it can be bitterly cold as well. Sounds very tough to say the least!

The Floating Green

Located in Coeur d'Alene in the upper Northwest part of Idaho, is The Coeur d'Alene Resort Golf Course with its famous 14th green. You may need to bring a few more golf balls as the par-3 14th hole is in the middle of a lake and is a very small island moveable by a system of cables that adjusts up to 218 yards long. The green is somewhat circular and roughly 15,000 square feet and accessed by a luxury ferry. [9]

Snow Golf (Ice Golf)

If 130 degrees is too hot for you, try the Uummannaq Golf Course in Qaasuitsup, Greenland which is the home of the World Ice Golf Championship.

The course is built on a giant iceberg and although the course is shorter than most golf courses, the golf cups to putt into are larger than normal. Don't use a white ball here. Yes, everything is frozen. The fairways are snow or ice instead of grass, and the greens are called "whites". [10]

Probably the greens here are faster than Augusta, but maybe not by much!

Grassless Golf Course

The Coober Pedy Opal Fields Golf Club in Southern Australia offers a unique golf experience. It was built in 1976 and you get a lot more distance with more roll here on the desert flats. The "greens" are black being oiled sand which provides a fairly smooth roll for putts. Some say this famous 18-hole par-72 course is just one big sand trap.

The course is on the desert flats and gibber hills of Coober Pedy. Opals are occasionally found on the grounds. [11]

Sad But Very True Golf Rules

Rule 1. It is easily possible to get worse no matter how badly you play.

Rule 2. Any change to correct your play is only effective for a maximum of one hole.

Rule 3. Bad shanks and shots come in consecutive groups of three. If you hit a fourth bad shot, it is really the beginning of your next group of three.

Rule 4. The more expensive the golf ball the easier it is to lose. Old and beaten up balls are usually impossible to lose.

Rule 5. Maintaining good swing thoughts. Try to keep no more than 98 swing thoughts in your head when you begin your takeaway.

Rule 6. Mistakes go to a secret place and come out at you unexpectedly. If you are driving the ball well, you will putt terribly. If you top it with your three metal, your irons will always get you there. When everything seems to be working, you'll get a blister from your golf shoes or step in animal crap.

Rule 7. The first thing every golfer does is fix a ball mark after making the green in regulation - even it rolls on. Every golfer also replaces the divot for every shot that makes the green in regulation.

Rule 8. Golf can best be defined as an endless series of misfortunes and aggravations which are totally forgotten by the occasional miracle shot, especially if you have a double Jack and an ice-cold beer after finishing.

Rule 9. Golf is extremely complicated. One day you'll hit every bunker, take two shots or more to get out of bunkers, slice every tee shot when you don't ever slice. Then, the next day, for no reason at all, you're golf really goes to hell.

Rule 10. If you're playing exceptionally well and very consistently, you must change your swing, or in the very least, your grip.

Rule 11. It's not difficult to hit a fairway if you don't care which fairway you hit.

Rule 12. If the drink cart girl pulls up while you're ready to tee off, you will whiff it, hit it OB, or dribble it short of the lady's tee. Don't be the slob that hits on her. Everyone does. Be a gentleman and she'll hit on you. Mostly for a good tip.

Rule 13. Be courteous to players in your group. Make sure you advise your opponent of all the pitfalls, penalty areas, wind factor, humidity factor, gators, etc. of the shot he is about to make.

Rule 14. Properly marking the ball most of the time results in shortening the putting distance.

Rule 15. The easiest shot in golf is a pitch over an extremely deep greenside bunker and hit it directly into the bunker.

Rule 16. The second easiest shot in golf is leaving the ball in the greenside bunker.

Rule 17. You lose new golf balls at a much faster rate (even if you are playing a wide-open and very well-manicured course with no penalty areas) as your supply of new balls decreases.

Rule 18. A golf lesson will relieve you of all your bad swing faults as well as your automatic compensating motions to correct bad swing faults.

Rule 19. A drunk golfer always has a better mental game than a sober player.

Rule 20.   Reversing the pre-shot routine. Use your actual swing as your practice swing, then use your practice swing to make your shot.

Rule 21. There are two things you can learn by stopping your backswing halfway to the top checking the position of your hands. The first thing is to determine how many hands you have, and the second thing is to determine which hand is wearing the glove.

Rule 22. If you want to hit your short irons as far as you could when you were 20 years younger, try to lay up short of a penalty area or a group of ladies in front of you.

Rule 23. If you think you have on your own figured out what you are doing wrong, that is precisely the exact thing you are doing right.

Rule 24. Frypan into the fire shot. When hit a bad shot don't look away or you'll miss your ball rolling into a hole and never find it.

Rule 25. The higher the handicap, the more the high handicap player knows about the how to make a correct golf swing and will always inform you how to correct your swing without you even asking.

Rule 26. When you lose a match on the 10th hole, you will win every hole after that.

Rule 27. 100-foot putts are generally made when you are lying 12 on the green.

Rule 28. Every golf hole has two types of bounces for the exact same shot. The first is an unfair and a totally unexpected bounce. The second is a bounce just the way you played it.

Rule 29. It is not difficult to hit a 2-inch leaf on a tree while it is extremely difficult to hit a fairway 100 yards wide.

Rule 30. All penalty areas are magnetized, and all fairways repel golf balls.

Rule 31. As you approach the green and see two balls one of which is just on a grassy edge of the sand trap and the other is almost completely buried in the trap, your ball is the one in the trap.

Rule 32. When there are two balls in the trap, your ball is a fried egg in the sand, or in a footprint and the other ball is sitting up nicely.

Rule 33. The track of a curving right to left putt with a six-foot break will always be followed by an uphill left to right putt with a twelve-foot of break.

Rule 34. It will always rain if you do not bring your umbrella and vice-versa.

Rule 35. You will always lose a club when playing with a brand new set, and the entire set is usually stolen if left in the rack on the first day you use them.

Rule 36. Golf carts will always run out of power the furthest distance from the pro shop.

Rule 37. You will always lose to the most annoying player in your foursome.

Rule 38. Hitting an iron off the tee will result in either totally missing the fairway or landing in a penalty area.

Rule 39. If you are approached by another golfer who wants to tell you all about how he shot 65, ask him to start with his final putt on the 18th.

Rule 40. When giving strokes, you always give too many. When you get strokes, you always don't get enough.

Rule 41. If you are playing well and your opponent tells you midway through the round you are a good player, you will always lose.

Rule 42. If you are playing badly and your opponent tells you are a bad player, you will always win.

Rule 43. The second you finish putting on your weather gear the rain will stop.

Rule 44. When playing an Ambrose format requiring all 4 players to have at least 3 drives, you will always be hitting your 3rd drive on the last hole that always has a lake and you will always hit into the lake.

Rule 45. You will play your best golf when there is nothing at stake or when you're not keeping score.

Rule 46. It is impossible to be consistent except when you hit your first drive OB and then hit your provisional ball to the exact same OB spot. Take no penalty for OB as it is not your fault. It is the golf course's fault for charging you a fee to play the course for which it did not buy enough property.

Rule 47. Velcro ripping, sneezing, coughing, and farting sounds must only be made on the backswing of other players.

Rule 48. Don't let another player attempt to hit a shot and interrupt your conversation.

Rule 49. Long approach shots that appear to stop six inches from the hole are always actually 20 feet away when you arrive at the green.

Rule 50. Hitting from a penalty area on the right side of the fairway always lands in a penalty area on the left side of the same fairway.

Rule 51. If you are paired up with a twosome in an important charitable or business-related tournament, you will always be paired with someone you just sued, and/or someone who slept with your wife before you were married.

Rule 52. You will always stub or chunk the first 70 shots after each golf lesson.

Rule 53. If you teach your wife, son, or daughter how to play golf, they will always beat you.

Rule 54. You should always expect a traffic jam, flat tire and/or a full parking lot when you are late for a tee time.

Rule 55. On blustery windy days, the wind will always be against you no matter what hole you are playing. The wind will always switch directions favorably when your opponent plays a shot.

Rule 56. On crowded weekends, the group in front of you is always slow and the group behind you is always fast.

Rule 57.   The shorter your putt is, the more the hole shrinks.

Rule 58. You will always hit your approach shot 50 feet or more away from the hole except when the green is under repair and there is a temporary green. In this case, you will always completely miss the temporary green and hit the ball one foot from the hole on the green under repair.

Rule 59. You will always find your ball if you put another ball in play before the three minute search time is up.

Rule 60. The more upscale the golf club is, the more balls will fall out of your bag when you lift it from your car.

Rule 61. The more upscale the golf club is, the looser your golf clubs will be strapped to the back of the cart and your golf bag will fall off exactly at the time when you want to impress someone.

Rule 61. If you are slicing all day and finally hit a drive down the middle on the final hole, your ball will roll and stop in a deep fairway divot.

Rule 62. The players behind you who hit into your group will always be bigger than any other player in your group.

Rule 63. The group you hit into will always be bigger than anyone in your group.

Rule 64. Golf courses are magically designed to have a toilet the furthest away when you must use them.

Rule 65. If you have several ways to play a shot, you will always choose the wrong way to play it.

Rule 66. The more you concentrate on an easy shot, the more difficult it becomes.

Rule 67. When you search for your ball you will find everyone else's ball except your own.

Rule 68. No matter how bad your last round of golf was, the worst is yet to come. This rule does not terminate on the 18th hole but will extend over your lifetime.

Rule 69. The more people you tell about the best round of golf you have ever played, the longer it will be before you ever get close to playing at that level again.

Rule 70. When you lose a match, talk very little. When you win a match, talk less.

Rule 71. Every player blames bad luck for bad shots but every player will always claim skill and sole responsibility for a hole-in-one.

Rule 72. If you call on God to improve your shot while the ball is in the air and the ball suddenly changes course or takes a favorable bounce, you are deemed to be using "an outside influence" and you must replace your ball to where it would have gone under the new rules of golf.

Rule 73. A ball will always come to rest halfway down a hill unless there are sand, high weeds, or water at the bottom of the hill and in that instance, the ball will continue on.

Rule 74. A good one iron shot is about as easy to come by as an understanding wife.

Rule 75. Talking to a golf ball won't do your game any good, unless you do it while your opponent is teeing off.

Rule 76. It is always fair not to take a penalty for a lost ball since a lost ball does not really exist - it will be found eventually.

Rule 77. It is always fair not to take a penalty for a lost ball if you are playing without the assistance of TV cameras and spotters like pro golfers.

Quotes About Golf

"My psychiatrist prescribed a game of golf as an antidote to the feelings of euphoria I experience from time to time."

- Bruce Lansky

Is this true? "Golf is said to be a humbling game, but it is surprising how many people are either not aware of their weaknesses or else reckless of consequences. Rhythm and timing are the two things which we all must have, yet no one knows how to teach either."

- Bobby Jones

"Art said he wanted to get more distance. So, I told him to hit it and run backward."

- Ken Venturi, re Art Rosenbaum

"I'm gambling that when we get into the next life, Saint Peter will look at us and ask, 'Golfer?' And when we nod, he will step aside and say, 'Go right in; you've suffered enough.' "One warning, if you do go in and the first thing you see is a par 3 surrounded by water, it ain't heaven."

- Jim Murray

"I can't wait to be that age and hanging out with a bunch of people hanging out all day playing golf and going to the beach, all my own age. We'd be laughing and having a good time and getting loopy on our prescription drugs. Driving golf carts around. I can't wait."

- Cameron Diaz

After Greg Norman lost the Masters. "When someone has a bad day like that on the golf course, you say, Greg, you look good, you look fantastic. I like your shoes, I like your pants, I like your...well, the hat's okay. I mean, you need to keep it light.

"Instead they say, 'Greg, what's next? Suicide? Alcoholism? Drugs?'"

- Bill Murray

"Golf is, in part, a game, but only in part. It is also in part a religion, a fever, a vice, a mirage, a frenzy, a fear, an abscess, a joy, a thrill, a pest, a disease, an uplift, a brooding, a melancholy, a dream of yesterday, and a hope for tomorrow."

- New York Tribune writer (1916)

"Reverse every natural instinct and do the opposite of what you are inclined to do, and you will probably come very close to having a perfect golf swing."

- Ben Hogan

"A golfer was heard mumbling to himself while counting his score after finishing a hole, 'I was on in two... then again in four...'"

- Brian Weiss

"The uglier a man's legs are, the better he plays golf. It's almost a law."

– H.G. Wells

"The number of shots taken by an opponent who is out of sight is equal to the square root of the sum of the number of curses heard plus the number of swishes."

- Michael Green

"Is my friend in the bunker or is the asshole on the green?"

- Anon.

"For a competitive junkie like me, golf is a great solution because it smacks you in the face every time you think you have accomplished something. That to me has taken over a lot of the energy and competitiveness for basketball."

- Michael Jordan

"Nice lag" should be translated as "Lousy putt."

Similarly, "Tough break" means, "Way to miss an easy one."

"That'll play" means, "Sh*tty shot, but we might be able to find it!"

- Anon.

"Golf is twenty percent mechanics and technique. The other eighty percent is philosophy, humor, tragedy, romance, melodrama, companionship, camaraderie, cussedness, and conversation."

- Grantland Rice

"The golf swing is like sex. You can't be thinking about the mechanics of the act while you are performing."

- Dave Hill, 13 PGA Tour Wins

"No matter what happens - never give up a hole... Tossing in your cards after a bad beginning you undermine your whole game, because to quit between tee and green is more habit-forming than drinking a highball before breakfast."

- Sam Snead

"Golf is the cruelest game, because eventually it will drag you out in front of the whole school, take your lunch money and slap you around."

- Rick Reilly

"We speak of eyeball-to-eyeball encounters between men great and small. Even more reaching and revealing of character is the eyeball-to-golfball confrontation, whereby our most secret natures are mercilessly tested by a small, round, whitish object with no mind or will but with a very definite life of its own, and with whims perverse and beatific."

- John Stewart Martin

"Golf is more fun than walking naked in a strange place, but not much."

- Buddy Hackett

"Another explanation for the 18-hole golf course has to do with whiskey. It takes just about 18 shots of whiskey to finish off a bottle. ... Scottish golfers took a shot of whiskey before playing each hole, so 18 shots brought about 18 holes on the course."

- Edwin Mike

"Got more dirt than ball. Here we go again. Then I thought, with the same clubhead speed, the ball's going to go at least six times as far. There's absolutely no drag, so if you do happen to spin it, it won't slice or hook 'cause there's no atmosphere to make it turn."

- Alan Shepard hitting a golf ball on the moon.

"It's harder to score well in a slow round. The tendency is to overthink shots while you're waiting and become mentally exhausted. Instead, chat with your playing partners about anything but golf. Concentrate on each shot for no more than a minute. You'll stay fresh."

- Rickie Fowler

"One of the most fascinating things about golf is how it reflects the cycle of life. No matter what you shoot - the next day you have to go back to the first tee and begin all over again and make yourself into something."

- Peter Jacobsen

"If your opponent is playing several shots in vain attempts to extricate himself from a bunker, and not giving up, do not stand near him and audibly count his strokes. It would be justifiable homicide if he wound up his pitiable exhibition by applying his niblick to your head."

- Harry Vardon

"The ball retriever is not long enough to get my putter out of the tree."

- Brian Weis

"Every golfer can expect to have four bad shots in a round and when you do, just put them out of your mind. This, of course, is hard to do when you've had them and you're not even off the first tee."

- Walter Hagan

"I'll tell you where it would be. Julius Boros would be a bookkeeper in Connecticut, Arnold Palmer would be in the Coast Guard, and I'd be back in Texas, picking cotton."

- Lee Trevino, on what the sport of golf would be like if there were no sponsorship money.

"Golf is a game in which a ball 1 1/2 inches in diameter is played on a ball 8,000 miles in diameter. The object is to hit the small ball, but not the larger."

- John Cunningham

"Why is golf exciting? Humans are stuck on the ground and for thousands of years, we learned how to launch projectiles. First, it was rocks. Skipping stones across water. Hurling stones off cliffs. Making things fly and watching where they land. Throwing spears. Shooting arrows. We love hitting things to make them fly. Likewise, golf is making something fly too, except we have grooves on the clubs and dimples on the ball to help us shape how the ball will fly. It's mesmerizing. People will spend hours at a golf practice range hitting balls and watching them fly. Over and over. Hundreds of balls. I'm not kidding."

- Don Stuart

"Half of golf is fun; the other half is putting."

- Peter Dobereiner

"The joy I get from winning a major championship doesn't even compare to the feeling I get when a kid writes a letter saying, 'Thank you so much. You have changed my life.'"

- Tiger Woods

"Telling me that I can't do something is probably the worst thing that anyone can say because I'll definitely do it. I'm very determined."

- Dustin Johnson

"One almost expects one of the players to peer into the monitor and politely request viewers to refrain from munching so loudly on cheese and crackers while the golfers are trying to reach the greens."

- Pete Alfano

"I never pray to God to make a putt. I pray to God to help me react well if I miss a putt."

- Chi-Chi Rodriguez

"Men who would face torture without a word become blasphemous at the short fourteenth. The game of golf may well be included in that category of intolerable provocations which may legally excuse or mitigate behavior not otherwise excusable."

- A.P. Herbert

"I shot one-under today. One under a tree, one under a bush, one under the water."

- Lee Trevino, relating how he scored one under for a round.

"The Supreme Court ruled that disabled golfer Casey Martin has a legal right to ride in a golf cart between shots at PGA Tour events. Man, the next thing you know, they're going to have some guy carry his clubs around for him."

- Jon Stewart

"Golf is a matter of confidence. If you think you cannot do it, there is no chance you will."

- Henry Colton

"The hole from hell is back ... If you don't drive a golf ball at least 268 yards, you will need the U.S. Navy on your left and the French Foreign Legion on the right."

- Edwin Pope

"I always think before an important shot: What is the worst that can happen on this shot? I can whiff it, shank it, or hit it out-of-bounds. But even if one of those bad things happens, I've got a little money in the bank, my wife still loves me, and my dog won't bite me when I come home."

- Byron Nelson

"If you pick up a golfer and hold it close to your ear like a conch shell and listen - you will hear an excuse."

- Fred Beck

"In Africa, some of the native tribes have a custom of beating the ground with clubs and uttering spine-chilling cries. Anthropologists call this a form of self-expression. In America, we call it golf."

- Ernest Becker

"I was shooting in the low 70s and 60s by the time I was twelve. That's the great thing about golf. It doesn't matter how old or young you are; if you're 90 and can shoot a good score, people will want to play with you."

- Bubba Watson

"Always keep in mind that if God didn't want a man to have mulligans, golf balls wouldn't come three to a sleeve."

- Dan Jenkins

"Counting on your opponent to inform you when he breaks a rule is like expecting him to make fun of his own haircut."

- Anon.

"The only sure rule in golf is he who has the fastest cart never has to play the bad lie."

- Mickey Mantle

"Any game where a man 60 can beat a man 30 ain't no game."

- Burt Shotten

"Senior golfers can discuss personal issues, reveal their personal secrets, and confess their most heinous sins and it really doesn't matter since no one cares or remembers what was said anyway."

- Anon.

"'I have to admit,' I said when he finished a lengthy discussion on the types of drivers, 'I've been golfing and it's about the most boring thing I've ever done. Old men drive around in golf carts pretending they're sporty and getting grouchy if there's any noise. It's like the nursing-home Olympics.'"

- Cindi Madsen, from "Cinderella Screwed Me Over"

"Playing golf is just like going to a strip club. You're all revved up, ready to go. But three hours later, you're depressed, plastered, and most of your balls are missing."

- James Clark

"We speak of eyeball-to-eyeball encounters between men great and small. Even more reaching and revealing of character is the eyeball-to-golfball confrontation, whereby our most secret natures are mercilessly tested by a small, round, whitish object with no mind or will but with a very definite life of its own, and with whims perverse and beatific."

- John Stewart Martin

It won't help to tell yourself not to hit it in the water as your mind only hears "water."

- Dr. Bob Rotella

"I met my wife through playing golf. She is French and couldn't speak English and I couldn't speak French, so there was little chance of us getting involved in any boring conversations - that's why we got married really quickly."

- Sean Connery

"One mid-afternoon on a sunny day, a golfer teed up his ball. He took a few practice swings and stepped up to his ball and took his stance getting ready to drive the first hole. As he was about to take the club away, a woman in a wedding gown frantically rushed up to him running like crazy from the parking lot. The woman is crying with tears streaming down her face. As she nears the first tee she screams, 'I can't believe it! How could you do this?'

"The golfer calmly took a swing and drove the ball straight down the middle of the fairway. He picked up his tee and turned to the woman and said, 'Hey...I said only if it's raining.'"

– Anon.

"A good one iron shot is about as easy to come by as an understanding wife."

- Dan Jenkins

"If I'm on the course and lightning starts, I get inside fast. If God wants to play through, let him."

- Bob Hope

"I used to play golf with a guy who cheated so badly that he once had a hole-in-one and wrote down zero on the scorecard."

- Bob Bruce

"It's the most humbling sport ever. It's like a lousy lover. It's like some guy who's never there when you need him. Occasionally, he comes and makes you feel like heaven on earth... And then the moment you say, 'I really need this,' he's gone."

- Dinah Shore

"Golf is like marriage: If you take yourself too seriously it won't work... and both are expensive."

- Anon.

"But in the end, it's still a game of golf, and if at the end of the day you can't shake hands with your opponents and still be friends, then you've missed the point."

- Payne Stewart

Go play golf.

Go to the golf course

Hit the ball

Find the ball.

Repeat until the ball is in the hole.

Have fun.

The end.

-Chuck Hogan

"We learn so many things from golf—how to suffer, for instance."

- Bruce Lansky

Golf Team Funny Names

Ever need a name for your foursome for tournaments, leagues, or other golf events? Check these out.

- **Lost Balls**
- **Par then bar**
- **Puff Caddie**
- **Angry Birdies**
- **Par tee on**
- **The Holey Ones**
- **I like Big Putts**
- **Grip It and Sip It**
- **Honor the Holes**
- **The Bogey Men**
- **Shanks for the Memories**
- **The Eagle Hunters**
- **Drunk by the Turn**
- **Chicks with Sticks**
- **The Ball Busters**
- **The Happy Hookers**
- **Where's the Beer Girl**
- **19th Holers**
- **The Shaft-Shank Redemption**

- **Complete and Putter Madness**
- **The Long Balls**
- **Young Tarts and Old Farts**
- **Respect All, Fear None**
- **This Putts for You**
- **#1 Balls in Golf**
- **Beer, Wings and Swings**
- **Lords of the Pins**
- **Meet the Putters**
- **The Big Sticks**
- **The Sons of Pitches**
- **Small Holes and Big Balls**
- **Plum Bob Snake Pants**
- **The Wonder Wackers**
- **Holes in Fun**
- **The Putter Nutters**
- **Designated Drivers**
- **Golftastics**
- **Golf Magicians**
- **Fore Play**
- **Fast Balls**
- **Couples Therapy**
- **Has Anyone Seen My Balls?**

Golf Jokes

My doctor told me to strengthen my cardio. He didn't care what exercise I did, he just told me to make sure I do any physical activity regularly that gets my heart rate elevated for 30 minutes at least 3 times a week.

In a month I saw him again. I told him I take 5 hour walks for 6 miles and walk through heavy bush and torrential rains. I go up and own hills, and I push my way through streams and lakes. I carry a 20 pound load and I fight off swarms of mosquitoes. I fight my way through tons of sand, digging, carrying turf, clearing branches, bend down repeatedly, walk in zig-zags, and almost collapse in total exhaustion at the end. I drink 5 beers afterwards to deal with the stress of it all.

"Wow!," the doctor said, "You are one hell of a hiker!"

"No," I replied. "I'm just a lousy golfer."

It was recently reported a golf ball has now been invented to automatically find and drop in the hole if it comes within 12 inches of the hole, but with a strong "WARNING: Do not carry this ball in your back pocket."

Many golf courses have a golf hole or two that are alongside busy streets with a lot of traffic.

At one of these holes, a golfer sliced his tee shot into oncoming moving traffic and the ball went through the windshield causing the driver to crash and be killed.

The driver's estate sued the golfer and a jury awarded the driver's estate a judgment for $40,000,000!

After the verdict, the Plaintiff's lawyer asked what the golfer was going to do about this?

The golfer replied, "Well, next time, I'm going to roll my right hand over more, so I can see at least two knuckles on my right hand."

After a tough round of golf, Joe walks into the golf clubhouse bar and reads a sign that hangs over the bar,

FREE BEER! FREE BEER FOR THE PERSON WHO CAN PASS THE TEST!

So, Joe asks the bartender what the test is.

The bartender says, "Well, first you have to drink that whole gallon of pepper tequila, the WHOLE thing at once and you can't make a face while doing it. Second, there's a 'gator out back with a sore tooth...you have to remove it with your bare hands. Third, there's a woman up-stairs who's never had an orgasm. You gotta make her have one and make things right for her."

Joe says, "Well, I've done some outrageous things in my life, but as much as I would love free beer, I won't do it. You have to be nuts to drink a gallon of pepper tequila and then it gets crazier from there."

Well, as time goes on Joe drinks a few, then he asks, "Wherez zat teeqeelah?" He grabs the gallon of pepper tequila with both hands and gulps it all down. Tears are now streaming down his face.

Next, he staggers out back, and soon all the people inside hear the most frightening roaring and thumping, and then silence. Joe staggers back into the bar, his shirt ripped, and big scratches were all over his body.

"Now," he says, "Where's that woman with the sore tooth?"

Golf courses sometimes have annoyances from wildlife such as bears, and players are advised by local wildlife control to be aware there are bears in the area. Golfers are advised to wear bells, whistles, or other noise devices to alert the bears of their presence and not startle them. Golfers are also advised to carry defensive pepper spray in case a bear should surprise them.

The authorities also try to make golfers aware of the presence of different bears such as the not so aggressive brown bear and the very aggressive grizzly bear. Golfers should know what brown bear droppings look like vs. grizzly bear droppings so they can be more alert of any potential danger.

Brown bear droppings are small and contain undigested nuts, and small animal fur.

Grizzly bear droppings usually have bells, whistles, and remnants of golf gloves, golf hats, and smell like pepper spray.

A father who had not played a game of golf with his 10-year-old son for several months, finally got him out to play on a Saturday morning.

On the first hole, the boy was hitting the ball into the woods, out of bounds, into ponds, and all over the place trying to play the first hole. He finally started to get his timing right and hit a beautiful shot to the first green and then sank a long putt.

"What was your score?" The father asked.

"4" replied the son.

"That's impossible. You must have hit more than 10 shots?"

"I only count the good ones."

Ernie Els died and was up before God for Judgment. He was met by St. Peter at the Gates of Heaven who greeted him.

"Mr. Els, you were a great golfer but before you meet God, I thought I should tell you that other than your great golf career, you really didn't do anything for the common good, or for the bad, so we're not sure what to do with you. We don't have any golf courses in heaven but what particularly did you do on earth that was good?"

Ernie pondered for a bit and said, "Once after playing a golf tournament in California, I was driving back to the hotel and there in the parking lot, I saw a young woman being tormented by a group of Hell's Angels – you know revving their engines, circling her, taunting her with obscenities?"

"Go on," said St. Peter.

"So, I stopped and got out of my car with my 5 iron and went up to the leader – the biggest guy there. He was much bigger than I, very muscular, had tattoos all over, a scar on his face and a ring in his nose. Well, I put my index finger in his nose ring and tore it out of his nose. Then I told him and the rest of them they'd better stop bothering this woman or they all would get more of the same!"

"Wow, that's very impressive Ernie!" St Peter replied. "When did this happen?"

"About two minutes ago."

Two couples were playing a foursome and the two men were very careful not to use any bad language. One man, however, was unfortunately, playing very badly, finding every sand trap, missing short putts, and finally sliced his ball terribly watching it splash into a large pond. Frustrated, he let out a wild and very loud string of curses!

The other man calmly said, "Careful, Joe, ladies are present."

"Sorry," Joe said.

The other man thought a bit and said, "Come to think about it, the best golfers on the planet play under huge pressure and yet you seldom hear them curse."

"Yeah, I guess you're right," Joe said. "But they are so good, what the f#ck do they have to bitch about?"

Three players were enjoying their usual Saturday golf round and came to the 3rd hole which was a par-4 severe dogleg left with a large water hazard all the way down the right side of the hole.

The first two players sliced their tee shot into the large water hazard and left the tee before the third player hit to try and hopefully find their balls. The first player went up to the water hazard and parted the waters and walked up to his ball and hit it within two feet of the cup.

The next player walked on top of the water hazard to exactly the spot where his ball went in the water, then sunk down, found his ball, and hit his ball within one foot of the cup.

The third player teed up then hit his ball in the middle of the fairway while the other two players were watching. Then the third player shanked his approach shot severely slicing it directly toward the water hazard when a bird caught it and dropped it into the cup.

Moses turned to Jesus and said, "I really hate playing golf with your Dad."

It's 1963, Jack Nicklaus is playing the final hole at The Masters on his way to his first Green Jacket. He hits a three wood off the tee just short of the bunker on the left side of the fairway and as he and his caddy are thinking over his next shot, Jack notices a snail going slowly past his ball. Not wanting to hurt the snail, he gently picks it up and walks over to the trees on the right side of the fairway and flings it into the woods.

It's now 1986, and Jack is again playing the final hole at Augusta on his way to winning his record 6th Green Jacket. While he and his caddie are looking over his second shot he sees a snail again slinking near his golf ball. He begins to bend down to pick up the snail and it happens to be the same snail from 23 years ago! The snail creeps halfway out of his shell, looks at Jack, and says, "What was that for?"

Grandpa is babysitting two of his grandkids. One of them asks, "Grandpa? What do you want for Grandparent's day?"

"All I want is your Grandma back."

"What?! Grandma is…?"

Grandpa interrupts. "Dead? No. She's out shopping, and I have a tee time in 30 minutes. How would the two of you like to ride around with me in a golf cart for five hours?"

A grandmother is giving directions to her grandson a professional golfer who took a week off from the tour to be with his wife and to visit his grandmother who he hadn't seen in a while.

Grandma tells him, "You come to the front door of the apartment. I am in apartment 301. There is a big panel at the front door. With your elbow, push button 301. I will buzz you in. Come inside, the elevator is on the right. Get in, and with your elbow, push 3. When you get out, I'm on the left. With your elbow, push my doorbell."

"Grandma, that sounds easy, but why am I hitting all these buttons with my elbow?"

"What! You're coming empty-handed?"

An old Italian man is dying. He calls his grandson who plays professional golf tournaments and travels a great deal. He tells him, "Alfredo, I wan' you lissina me. I wan' you to take-a my chrome plated .38 revolver so you will always remember me."

"But grandpa, I really don't like guns. How about you leave me your Rolex watch instead?"

"You lissina me, boy. Somma day you gonna be traveling around and you gonna have a beautiful wife, lotsa money, a big-a home and maybe a couple of bambinos. And, somma day you gonna come-a home and maybe finda you wife inna bed with another man.

Whatta you gonna do then? Pointa to you Rolex watch and say, 'times up?'"

A father, son & grandfather were about to tee off when a beautiful young woman walked up and asked if she could join them. Without hesitation, they all agreed.

The young woman thanked them and said, "I appreciate you letting me join but please do not try and give me tips throughout the round. All of them agreed and they all teed off.

As the round went on all three men were impressed as the woman played golf beautifully. When they got to the 18th green, the young woman says, "You guys have been great today none have you have tried to coach me in any way you just let me play. Now, I'm going to show my appreciation. If I sink this final putt, this score will be a new personal best for me. But I think I need some advice on

44

the line of this putt and if anyone can help me make it, I will give you anything you want."

Immediately, the grandson gets down low to the ground and starts reading the green. Then says 6 inches right nice and easy you'll make this putt."

The father then tries to read the putt and says, "Right edge of the cup and it's yours."

The grandfather walks over picks up the ball and tosses it back to her and says, "That's a gimme."

Jack and his wife Jane are celebrating their 40th wedding anniversary in the fancy golf clubhouse dining room. They toast to each other and as they put their glasses down, Jack asks her, "Jane after all these years, I was wondering if you ever were unfaithful to me."

"Oh, Jack, I don't want to talk about…"

"Jane, I really want to know."

"Oh, alright. Three times."

"Three? Okay, when were they?"

"Well Jack, remember when we first got married you really needed a loan to start your business and no bank would touch you? Well, remember the chief bank loan officer came over to the house with a check for you, and had you sign all the loan papers?"

"Oh, Jane, you did that for me? I think even more of you now...but when was the second time?"

"Remember when you had your heart attack and were close to death? No one wanted to operate on you. Then the best cardiac surgeon in town suddenly appeared and operated on you?"

"Oh, gosh Jane, I love you so much. You saved my life. So, when was the third time?"

"Well, Jack, remember last year when you wanted to be golf club captain and you were 27 votes short?"

Several golfers are in the locker room getting ready to play when they hear a mobile phone on a bench ring. One of the guys picks it up and answers it. Everyone else in the locker room stops to listen.

Golfer: Hello?

Woman: Hi Honey, it's me are you at the club?

Golfer: Yes.

Woman: I'm at the mall and found this beautiful coat. It's only $900. Okay if I buy it?

Golfer: Sure, go ahead if you really like it.

Woman: I stopped at the Jaguar dealership and they've got a brand new F-Type in and I really like it.

Golfer: How much is it?

Woman: $70,000.

Golfer: Well okay buy it but make sure you get all the options.

Woman: Fantastic! Oh, one more thing. The house we saw last year is back on the market and they dropped the price to $1.1 million.

Golfer: Well go ahead and offer $1,050,000 and see if they take it. If not give them full price.

Woman: That's great! Will do. I love you, honey. You are so good to me!

Golfer: Well you're worth every penny. Love you too. Bye.

The golfer hangs up. The other guys in the locker room are speechless and staring at him with their mouths open.

The golfer looks at them and says, "Anybody know whose phone this is?"

Four ladies are playing golf when a streaker with a brown paper bag painted with a yellow smiley face covering his head jogged slowly past them showing everything he had leaving nothing to the imagination.

The first woman says, "Oh my God! That's incredible! What nerve! I'm going to call the police!"

The second woman says, "I couldn't recognize him in a lineup. I was focused on looking at something else and that wasn't my husband!"

The third lady says, "Why he didn't even resemble any of our husbands!"

The fourth lady says, "The nerve of that guy! Why he doesn't even belong to this club!"

Dear Abby,

I've never written to you before, but I really need your advice. I have suspected for some time now that my wife has been cheating on me. The usual signs. Phone rings but if I answer, the caller hangs up. My wife has been going out with "the girls" a lot recently although when I ask their names she always says, "Just some friends from work, you don't know them."

I always try to stay awake to look out for her coming home, but I usually fall asleep. Anyway, I have never approached the subject with my wife. I think deep down I just didn't want to know the truth, but last night she went out again and I decided to really check on her. Around midnight, I decided to hide in the garage behind my golf clubs so I could get a good view of the whole street when she arrived home from a night out with "the girls."

It was at that moment, crouching behind my clubs, that I noticed that the graphite shaft on my driver appeared to have a hairline crack right by the clubhead.

Is this something I can fix myself or should I take it back to the pro shop where I bought it?

Signed,

Perplexed

Simon forgot his wedding anniversary and his wife was ticked off at him.

She told him, "Tomorrow morning, I expect to find a gift in the driveway that goes from 0 to 200 in under 6 seconds, AND IT BETTER BE THERE."

The next morning, Simon got up early.

When his wife woke up a couple of hours later, she looked out the window, and sure enough, there was a small gift-wrapped box sitting in the middle of the driveway.

Confused, the wife put on her robe, ran out to the driveway, and took the box into the house.

She opened it and found a brand-new bathroom scale.

Simon is not yet well enough to have visitors.

PGA Tour Players spend 90% of the year travelling from one tournament to another and spend a lot of time on airplanes.

On an Air India Flight to the US carrying 103 passengers, the crew unfortunately discovered 30 minutes into the flight there were only 40 meals on the plane.

One very clever crew member came up with a solution and announced, "I'm very sorry, and we don't know how this happened, but we have 103 passengers and only 40 dinners on this plane."

After the loud muttering amongst the passengers quieted down, she continued, "Anyone who is kind enough to give up their dinner so someone else could eat, will receive unlimited free alcoholic beverages during the entire duration of the flight."

A second announcement was made an hour and a half later, "If anyone wants to change their mind, we still have 40 dinners available."

True Golf Stories

The Competitive Nature of Tiger Woods

What made Tiger a superstar? In November 1990, he was interviewed at the age of 14 and was able to drive over 300 yards and a scratch golfer. The interviewer asked Tiger, what did he think made him such a great golfer.

Tiger simply said, "It's my competitiveness. By that I mean, when you must make a putt or a shot, you drop into a zone and do it." [12]

In 2015, when Tiger returned to golf after several back operations, he said, "Competing is still the same. I'm trying to beat everybody out there. That hasn't changed. I prepare to win and expect to go and do that... The only difference is that I won The Masters when Jordan Spieth was still in diapers." [13]

Tiger has often been quoted many times about his desire to compete. "As a kid, I might have been psycho, I guess, but I used to throw golf balls and get them stuck in the trees and then try and somehow make par from them. I thought that was fun."

"People don't understand that when I grew up, I was never the most talented. I was never the biggest. I was never the fastest. I certainly was never the strongest. The only thing I had was my work ethic, and that's been what has gotten me this far."

Snakes on the Course

A judge in Florida heard a Motion to Dismiss on a complaint of a golfer who'd been bitten by a rattlesnake looking for his ball in the rough and later filed suit against the golf course for damages.

The snake-bitten Plaintiff's lawyer argued, "Your honor, the golf course should have had, in the very least, a simple warning sign, "Beware of poisonous snakes."

The judge considered it a second, then said, "If I rule the Plaintiff has a right to sue in this case, then that would require every golf course in the State to post a sign, 'Beware of Rattlesnakes.' Well, everyone knows there are poisonous snakes in this state. Do hammer manufacturers have to put labels on hammers – 'If you hit your thumb with this, it will hurt you?' Case dismissed."

Mystery Pooper

At the Stavanger Golf Club in Norway, golf maintenance found loo paper and human turds in a variety of golf holes. They figured it must be a man doing it since the turds were too large for a woman. There were also bicycle tracks traced in the morning dew that they followed. There were also male footsteps from the bicycle tracks to the pooped golf hole and back again. The bicycle tracks then left the same way.

The pooper used a variety of holes to confuse course maintenance and avoid being caught. Most of the time used toilet paper would be found with the turds and some turds were found in holes with no toilet paper. The scratchy pooper probably got a seat on busses very easily.

The golf course installed lights, but the pooper apparently skillfully cut the power to the lights risking his own electrocution in the dark of night.

To this day the pooper has not been apprehended. Some speculate these nefarious deeds were caused by a smelly disgruntled electrician who doesn't like this particular golf course.

Groundskeepers have been perplexed trying to determine the pooper's intentions on why he has been doing this for so long without being apprehended. The Managing Director of the club concluded, the pooper most likely hates the game of golf or may have mental issues. [14]

Phil Mickleson

"Phil is brilliant, but he's nuts. There's something not quite right about that boy. Phil is watching a movie that only Phil can see.

His mother told me, 'Phil was so clumsy as a little boy, we had to put a football helmet on him until he was 4 because he kept bumping into things.'

I told her, 'Mary, Mary, I'm a writer, you can't keep handing me material like this.'

So, the next time I saw Phil I said, 'You didn't really wear a football helmet in the house until you were 4, did you?"

He said, 'It was more like 5.'"

-David Feherty on Phil Mickleson

I Wouldn't Do That Mate

A tourist was playing a golf course in Northern Queensland. After hitting his drive to the right of the fairway into the rough where there were tall grasses and bushes, the tourist golfer drove his cart to where his ball went and walked into the bush looking for his ball.

The two Aussies he was playing drove up fast with one of them shouting, "Hold on, mate!"

"It's okay, I'm just going to take a quick look for my ball."

The Aussies began chuckling.

"What?" The tourist asked.

"That's a funnel-web spider right next to your arm, mate. There's a female spider on the web and there should be a male somewhere on the ground."

"Are they dangerous?"

Both Aussies were laughing now, "You've got to respect the nature here, mate." (Note: Funnel-web spiders are highly poisonous and shown on the next page).

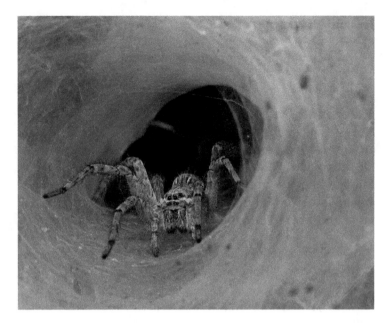

Images from Creative Commons

Golfer Attack and Brawl

The Associated Press reported, two golfers received jail sentences for attacking two people, a father, and his son, while they were playing the Rose City Golf Course in Portland, Oregon. [15]

The two men apparently were drunk and playing the golf course in the wrong direction. The father and his son called out to them trying to tell them they were playing the course backward.

After encountering each other a second time, the two men struck the father and the son with golf clubs. The father and the son were injured and suffered cuts and broken fingers but they, with the help of another man, were able to subdue the drunken men until police arrived.

The two men received jail time and probation for assault. One of the defendants claimed he was so drunk he didn't remember anything. They also both paid for several hundred dollars for the damages they did and were ordered to take anger management classes as part of their sentence. [16]

Golf Club "Mean Girl" Clique

The social life at a golf club can be a lot of fun but things got out of hand in July 2016 at the Buckingham Golf Club in beautiful British Countryside just North of London.

It was allegedly reported in the Daily Mail [17] that one member, Kaye, was in a relationship with Columb

Harrington, the older brother of Padraig Harrington, and Kaye was accused of falsifying her handicap. Kaye complained to the club about the false accusations.

That didn't do much good since soon after she complained, she got an anonymous letter posted on her club locker, "You bitch."

The clique of women who didn't like Kaye allegedly didn't want to stop there. Kaye later received an anonymous letter at her home, "If you're so unhappy perhaps you should join another club. We would like you to. You just like trouble."

Kaye boldly responded on her Facebook page saying she knew some of the lady members didn't like her, "and I secretly know this, and I don't give a F#ck."

After a few weeks, someone smashed a window at the back of Kaye's home using a golf club. Yes, it seems you must be mean to spend your time doing things like that.

The police were contacted to investigate and sent out an officer to let the clique of senior ladies know they cannot go around bullying and harassing people giving them an appropriate warning. Yes, that officer is still alive today and survived the ordeal and bravely put an end to it.

Playing Through Can be Dangerous

According to the Oklahoma Channel 4 News, [18] the Edmond Oklahoma police were called to stop a brawl at the Kickingbird Golf course. A 55-year-old single-player (who was also a diagnosed paranoid schizophrenic) asked if he could play through a foursome of golfers ahead of him. One person in the foursome, a 67-year-old, took exception and they got into a war of words winding up standing nose to nose arguing.

The single-player took a step back because his mental condition makes him extremely nervous when someone gets into his bubble. The single-player was then hit on the top and front of his head with a putter.

Another member of the foursome, a 72-year-old, hit the single-player in the butt and legs while the single-player was at the same time being hit in the head with a putter by the 67-year-old.

The single-player had to have staples and 10 stitches in his head.

Both assailants were arrested and charged with assault and battery with a dangerous weapon even though they claimed the single player started it.   The prosecutor disregarded who started it due to the serious injuries to the single-player.

Mysterious Free Golf Balls

According to the LebTown News, for two years an unknown person has been leaving golf balls on the streets of Lebanon, Pennsylvania. Some of the free golf balls are Pro V1s considered to be the best golf balls. The balls aren't causing damage to anyone and the residents are picking them up and using them when they play golf. The residents want to thank whoever is doing this, but the mysterious golf ball Santa identity is unknown. [19]

Beware Hitting Into Someone's Yard

Ever hit your shot into someone's yard? According to KDKA CBS Pittsburg, a man pulled a handgun on a golfer trying to retrieve his golf ball from his yard. There wasn't any report on whether he got his golf ball back or not, but the homeowner was arrested and charged with terroristic threats, simple assault, and harassment.   The golfer probably stopped playing to change his underwear. [20]

Playing too much golf and ignoring the wife?

The TV news reported in Yeosu, South Korea, a South Korean golfer had his penis cut off by his wife while he slept. The man was heard groaning by a neighbor in the next apartment and found him bleeding and lying on the floor. The wife was arrested.

In her own defense, she explained her husband continually ignored her, had been violent toward her, gave her no money while he went out and played golf all the time.

The husband was hospitalized, and the investigation continued. [21]

North Korean Golf Gag

Is your golf life getting dull? According to Nine News in Australia, two young Aussies (one a builder and the other a real estate agent) were playing in a polo tournament in Beijing, China, and heard about a pro tournament in North Korea. As a gag, they tried to enter and surprisingly learned they were allowed to play as the tournament officials apparently mistook them to be the Australian team.

As it turned out, they were exposed by their own lack of skill as one of them shot 120 (and yet he came in next to last), but they could leave North Korea thankfully.

So, after being allowed to leave North Korea, which might have been a place they might have not ever returned from, you would think they learned their lesson. However, one of them announced they just heard the Somalian National Golf Open was coming up and they were going to try to enter it. [22]

Wild and Crazy Golf Tournament

KMOV 4 TV News in Columbia, Illinois reported a "Charity Golf Tournament" got out of hand and the tournament organizer was charged with deceptive practices for allegedly misrepresenting the tournament as a charity event.

As it turned out several beautiful women in bikinis were entertaining the golfers with alleged nudity and sex acts, but unfortunately, no money was apparently raised for charity. [23]

Another Wild and Crazy Golf Tournament

Is the PGA Tour losing viewers?   Here's a possible solution. CBS News reported strippers and players were having too much fun at the Pink Monkey Golf Outing (the Pink Monkey is a Chicago strip club).

It was reported by CBS News that one grandmother said, "There was a lot of nudity and things that don't belong on a public golf course." The golf course, Bensenville's White Pines Golf Club, has homes nearby and locals were seen taking pictures of the antics going on. [24]

Amazing Husband and Wife Hole Out

The Lansing State Journal reported an amazing story of a husband and wife who on consecutive shots made a hole in one while playing on a Sunday afternoon that was verified by witnesses.

The husband first teed up at the par 3 16th hole at Ledge Meadows Golf Course in Grand Ledge, Michigan, and aced it. Then his wife immediately followed the husband's ace by teeing up making her ace on the same hole. [25]

Duffer Tees Up on Duff Cheeks

TMZ News reported Liz Dickson, a model, sued Playboy, and settled for an undisclosed sum during the Playboy Golf Finals when a ball was teed up in her butt crack and she was inadvertently struck by the club on the downswing striking her butt cheek causing a massive welt and other problems. Something definitely not to be tried at home. [26]

The Rest of the Foursome to the Rescue

At the Iberostar Cancun Golf Club, in Cancun Mexico, the Daily Record reported a Scottish man was bitten and dragged by a large crocodile living on the course and probably would have been eaten if not for the others in his foursome who came quickly to his rescue.

The Scottish man was playing a shot from a bunker when the croc bit into him and dragged him a bit. One of the others came to his rescue and began beating the croc with a 9 iron. The other two instinctively joined in the rescue by driving their golf cart over the 12-foot croc until the hungry croc released the man. [27]

Police Stop 8 Man Club Swinging Brawl

According to the Birmingham Live News, an 8 man brawl erupted on the Greenway Hole Golf Club in Stockton Brook England. [28]

Police were called and on their own initiative drove in golf carts to the location of the brawl still in progress on the course which reportedly started over a slow play issue. Charges were filed against 4 men but were later dropped.

The officers riding to break up the fracas drove the golf carts as fast as they could and got there (without any emergency flashing lights) and quickly calmed everyone down.

The police reported there were minor injuries and broken bones from weapons used in the fight.

News reported Chief Inspector John Owen, said, "I'm very proud of my officers. They've used initiative, gone to a fight outnumbered, and have resolved it resulting in peace and order. Hole in one I'd say!"

Guinness Book Record for the Longest Drive

Mike Austin hit a 516-yard drive in 1974 at the Winterwood Golf Course. This was recorded at the US Senior National Open Qualifier event. He used a driver with a 43.5-inch steel-shafted persimmon wood driver.

Although not a record, Louis Oosthuizen hit a 500-yard drive with the help of a cart path in 2013 during the second round of the Ballantine's Championship in Korea. The endnote in this book references the YouTube where you can view this colossal and time-consuming drive. [29]

Although not in Guinness, probably the longest drive occurred in 1992, by a man named Carl Cooper who hit his drive 787 yards on the 3rd Hole of the second round of the 1992 Texas Open at Oak Hills Country Club. His drive landed on a concrete cart path angled downhill. The ball took a huge bounce down the path for a total of 787 yards from its original destination. Since his ball went way past the green, he wound up scoring a double bogey!

Guinness Book Record for the Longest Putt

There are two 110 foot putts on record as the longest putts known. The first was made by Jack Nicklaus in the 1964 Tournament of Champions played at the Desert Inn Country Club in Las Vegas. The second 110 footer by Nick Price in the 1992 PGA Championship at Bellerive Country Club near St. Louis, Missouri.

By the way, Jack made a "shorter" one in front of a crowd of spectators that was only 102 feet long while showing Johnny Miller how to make a long putt. [30]

The Highest Single Hole Score in a Major

Ever feel bad for taking a high score on a hole? The worst PGA tour score on a golf hole in a major tournament occurred in 1938 by Ray Ainsley's on the 16th hole, a par 4 at Cherry Hills GC during the 1938 U.S. Open in second-round play.

Ray hit his approach shot into a creek. An issue arose in Ray's mind since he wasn't sure of the rules and thought he had to play the ball where it lies. The ball kept moving because of the current in the creek. Despite the moving ball, Ray kept trying to hit it before it would move farther away. He'd make contact and the ball would shoot in the air only to hit the bank and roll back into the water. He finally got it out but hit the ball over the green behind a tree. A score of 19 was posted on his card which he signed but he was reported to have had a record 23 strokes on the hole. He shot a 96 for the round and missed the cut.

Guinness Record for the Lowest 72 Hole Score

The lowest score to par after 72 holes in a major golf tournament is 32 under par (total of 256 for four rounds) by Chapchai Nirat a pro from Thailand at the 2009 SAIL Open at the Classic Golf Resort, in Gurgaon, India. This happened on March 21, 2009, and he began the tournament with two rounds of 62 followed by a 65 and finished the fourth round with a 67. The SAIL Open is (according to the International Federation of PGA Tours) a "major" tournament. [31] This 72 hole total beat Ernie Els' 31-under-par when he won the 2003 Mercedes-Benz Championship by eight shots at Kapalua. Kapalua is a par 73 course.

Also, Dustin Johnson set a new PGA Tour record for the lowest score on a par-71 course at 30 under over 72 holes in 2020 at the Northern Trust Open in Boston. Steve Stricker in 2009 was 33 under par at a 90 hole Bob Hope Classic. [32]

Longest Golf Ball Carry below 1000 meters

What is the record for the longest flight of a golf ball in the air below an altitude of 1000 meters, i.e. an altitude below

3,280 feet? Ryan Winther on July 12th, 2012 using a Krank Rage 6 Driver with a 46-inch shaft and 6-degree loft, hit a golf ball and the ball stayed in the air for 430 yards or 292.19 meters. Ryan was a former long ball drive champion and currently holds this ball flight world record. [33]

Fastest 4-Ball Round

Does slow play bother you? It bothers most every golfer. The fastest golf round by four players playing as a foursome were Matthew Dalton, Steven Holloway, Landyn Edwards and Michael Ryan (all Kiwis) completed 18 holes in 48 min 56 sec at Rotorua Golf Club, Rotorua, New Zealand, on 12 November 2017.

The record was attempted and successfully set as part of a fundraiser. [34]

Break a Golf Guinness Book of Record

If your life is boring and you want to go into the Guinness Book of Records, check out the numerous records they list on their site at Guinness World Records.com. There are numerous records ranging from the longest time controlling a ball on a golf club to the fastest round of golf by a robot. [35]

Mental Game: How to Deal with that Annoying Golfer

The overwhelming majority of golfers are wonderful and perfect gentlemen and great to play golf with. But what should you do with the one guy or girl who gets under your skin? You know, the one who makes snide remarks after you make a bad shot, walks on your putting line, fiddles with his clubs while you're swinging, etc.

You know everyone isn't perfect in the world and most people are polite, but generally playing with an annoying player is bound to occur. Here are four very simple suggestions on what to do. The first suggestion comes from Tiger Woods who probably has more distractions than most golfers considering the crowds that follow him.

Suggestion 1. Tiger Woods related a well-known story about how his dad, Earl, use to make loud noises, toss clubs, and generally distract Tiger when he was hitting. He was overly extreme in making noises, etc. since he wanted Tiger to be able to handle distractions or than anything that could disrupt his play on the course. Earl wanted Tiger to be able to focus regardless of distractions, so he taught Tiger mental toughness. In this spirit, try keeping cool and focused and strengthen your mental toughness. Practice hitting on the range regardless of what is going on around you.

Suggestion 2. If annoyances occur while you are taking back the club before hitting the ball, practice how to stop your takeaway, upswing, and downswing before striking the ball. Have a friend purposely make noise or otherwise distract you on the range while you are swinging.

Suggestion 3. Etiquette errors. If another player in your group breaks rules of etiquette, politely inform them of it for their own good. At the same time, view this is as an opportunity for you to strengthen your good manners by keeping cool and controlling your emotions when dealing with bad manners.

Suggestion 4. Most rounds of golf are fun with very well-mannered people. If an annoyance starts by a player on the first few holes, it's a good idea to call it to the person's attention firmly and politely so it doesn't get worse as the game progresses.

A few examples of annoying golfers.

1. The "Asinine Advice guy" has a handicap of 28 + and freely gives advice even though no one is asking. Also known for telling everyone what he did wrong after each missed shot.

2. The "Put me down for a 4 grifter guy" says after taking too many shots. Known for stopping strangers and shoving his card in their noses. Has infinite excuses why the other guy forgot to sign.

3. The "Club throwing anger management dropout guy." Puts everyone on edge. People get ready to duck when he duffs a shot. Usually found around ponds on the course trying to retrieve his clubs.

4. "Cigar and beer guy." Has a steady lit cigar, cigar holder, fancy blow torch lighter, brass cigar cutter, and an open extra-tall beer can in the drink holder. Is known to create large smoke clouds above the half-way house while telling tales. Looks sober most of the time. Easy to spot if you hear, "A few beers oil the hinges, you know."

5. The "Ballhawk guy." Stops at every penalty area searching for balls. Finds a yellowed, cut Pro V and tells you how much they cost. Searches for 15 minutes for his ball while telling you how many others he found.

6. The "Dreamer guy." Has a 28+ handicap. Usually seen on par 5 fairways 300 yards from the green taking practice swings waiting for players on the green to finish. Then hits it 60 yards after green is clear. Usually says things like, "You never know."

7. "Mr. Mulligan." You can tell he's around when you see him reaching into his pocket or going back to his bag and hearing, "I'm going to hit one more," repeatedly while his playing partners moving ahead without him.

8. "Always finds his ball guy." You can tell he's around when you hear, "I don't want to hold you up, I'll find it. You guys go ahead." Known to have holes in the pockets of his long pants and calls out, "It's still in bounds!"

9. "Ego handicapper guy." Has a 9 handicap yet shoots 101 regularly. Known to say, "I'm off today," or "I'm not turning in *this* card." Tells unwanted tall tales of his fake ability and amazing golf shots. Known to have trouble finding people to play golf with him.

10. Mr. Rangefinder. Holds up play. Figures his own and everyone else's distance. You know he's around when you hear, "Wait, I can tell you exactly how far it is," especially when the pin is in the middle of the green and you are right at the 150 yard marker.

11. "Loquacious Larry guy" who talks too much usually about stuff he's only interested in. Exception, joke telling at the right time is fine. Lee Trevino is well-known for his joke telling talent.

Jack Nicklaus: "I don't want to talk today, Lee."

Lee Trevino: "That's OK, Jack. You don't have to talk; you just have to listen!"

12. The "Slow-go golfer guy." Over concentrates on everything. He's totally relaxed while night begins to fall while you tense up watching the backup building behind you. Usually oblivious to everything. Has been known to be repeatedly stuck with bar tabs while his buddies quietly leave when he's pontificating on how well he played.

Quick Jokes for the Mental Game

Enough of the "4 semi-serious suggestions" from the previous chapter. Consider these one or two liners for a quick laugh.

Play the ball where it lies unless you got f#cked by your ball unluckily rolling into a fairway divot, behind a bush, etc. Feel free to nudge it out when no one's looking.

Putts less than 2 feet are always gimmies.

A "friendly wager" does not exist playing golf no matter what the amount is.

Any form of wagering makes short putts longer and drives shorter.

Only very foolish men attempt to give golf lessons to their wives.

When you must hit over water from the tee, don't wash your ball before teeing it up.

It takes playing at least 15 holes to warm up.

Fast players never play on weekends.

There are only three sure ways to improve your golf score,

1) Take lessons,

2) Practice more,

3) Start cheating.

You have serious issues if you know there is more to life than golf, but you are not interested in finding out.

Golf balls are very similar to eggs. Both are white and sold by the dozen and you're always buying more.

The easiest way to slice a ball is to try and hook it.

Why are tour players overheated when playing during the pandemic crisis?

A. There are no fans on the course.

And remember always, every golf match is a test of your great golf skill and experience versus your opponent's luck.

A Final Message

We hope you enjoyed this book. If you liked it, please take a minute to leave a short review on Amazon or Goodreads. Thank you.

TeamGolfwell.com

Other Books by Team Golfwell

Rules of Golf: A Handy Fast Guide to Golf Rules

Golf Shots: How to Easily Hit a Wide Variety of Shots like Stingers, Flop Shots, Wet Sand Shots, and Many More for Better Scoring

A Complete Guide for Golfers Over 50: How to Reach Your Full Playing Potential and Have Fun Doing It

Brilliant Screen-Free Stuff to Do with Kids: A Handy Reference for Parents & Grandparents!

GOLF: It's Like Life Itself. Amusing Golf Quotes & Stories

The Funniest Quotations to Brighten Every Day: Brilliant, Inspiring, and Hilarious Thoughts from Great Minds

Walk the Winning Ways of Golf's Greatests: How the Greatest Players in Golf Found Inspiration to Win and Their Advice to Young Golfers

Golf's New Rules: A Handy Fast Reference

Great Golf Formats: Golf Betting Games, and More Hilarious Adult Golf Jokes and Stories

Jokes for Very Funny Kids (Big & Little): A Treasury of Funny Jokes and Riddles Ages 9 - 12 and Up
And many more at TeamGolfwell.com

And many more here

References

[1] Nullarborlink Golf Course, the longest course in the world, http://www.nullarborlinks.com/course

[2] Guinness World Records, https://www.guinnessworldrecords.com/world-records/longest-golf-course

[3] Harris Kalinka, http://harriskalinka.com/blog/the-worlds-deepest-bunker/

[4] Legend Golf and Safari Resort, https://www.legendvillage.co.za/

[5] La Jenny, Naturist Golf Course, https://www.lajenny.fr/en/activities-and-entertainment-in-the-naturist-village-la-jenny/naturist-golf-course-near-bordeaux/

[6] Sikkim Tourism, http://www.sikkimtourism.gov.in/Webforms/General/pdf/YAK_Golf_Course.pdf

[7] Copper Colorado Golf Club, https://www.coppercolorado.com/golf/book-a-tee-time/public

[8] Furnace Creek Golf Course, https://www.oasisatdeathvalley.com/furnace-creek-golf-course/

[9] Coeur d'Alene Resort, https://www.cdaresort.com/gallery/golfcourse

[10] Wikipedia, Snow Golf, https://en.wikipedia.org/wiki/Snow_golf

[11] Coober Pedy Opal Fields Golf Club, http://www.cooberpedygolfclub.com.au/

[12] YouTube, Trans World Sports, https://www.youtube.com/watch?v=2dHjdiT6wgA&feature=youtu.be

[13] Business Insider Australia, Tiger's Extraordinary Competitiveness, https://www.businessinsider.com.au/tiger-woods-competitiveness-2015-4?r=US&IR=T

[14] United Press International, July 24, 2015, https://www.upi.com/Odd_News/2015/07/24/Mystery-pooper-targeting-holes-of-Norwegian-golf-course/2881437763634/

[15] Associated Press International, Drunken golfers sentenced after attacking others with clubs, February 15, 2019, https://www.koin.com/news/crime/drunken-golfers-sentenced-after-attacking-others-with-clubs/1784318547/

[16] Ibid.

[17] Daily Mail, https://www.dailymail.co.uk/news/article-3681389/Police-probe-feuding-golfers-vile-taunts-smashed-window-poison-pen-letters-rock-local-club.html

[18] Oklahoma Channel 4 News, June 1, 2018, https://www.golfdigest.com/story/man-gets-beaten-with-putter-after-asking-to-play-through-foursome-at-oklahoma-golf-course

[19] LebTown News, https://lebtown.com/2020/07/02/2-years-of-random-palmyra-golf-balls-and-no-answer-to-mystery-in-sight/

[20] KDKA CBS Pittsburg, https://pittsburgh.cbslocal.com/2018/09/16/butler-man-threatened-pistol-golf-ball/

[21] MBN News, http://m.jejuweekly.com/news/articleView.html?idxno=5526

22 NINE News, https://streamable.com/07zn

23 KMOV 4 News, https://www.kmov.com/news/event-billed-as-charity-golf-tournament-turns-x-rated/article_c3ae5076-c63f-5216-a962-6ffc8affb361.html

24 CBS News Chicago, http://www.cbsnews.com/news/strippers-cavort-at-public-golf-course-in-chicago/

25 Lansing State Journal, https://www.lansingstatejournal.com/story/sports/2015/05/27/rare-holes-one/28026961/

26 TMZ News, https://www.tmz.com/2014/03/15/liz-dickinson-playboy-golf-swing-ass-cheek-lawsuit/

27 Daily Record, https://www.dailyrecord.co.uk/news/scottish-news/golfers-mexican-resort-describe-moment-2786025

28 Birmingham Live News, April 26, 2016, https://www.birminghammail.co.uk/news/midlands-news/brawl-breaks-out-golf-course-14580119

29 YouTube, European Tour, https://www.youtube.com/watch?v=QXq-ZTPpRQ4

30 YouTube, PGA, https://www.youtube.com/watch?v=u9KrMQDU94g

31 Guinness World Records, https://www.guinnessworldrecords.com/world-records/lowest-score-under-par-in-a-professional-golf-tour-tournament

32 The Post and Courier, Myrtle Beach, https://www.postandcourier.com/myrtle-beach/former-coastal-carolina-star-dustin-johnson-returns-to-world-no-1-sets-pga-tour-record/article_292e561a-e58e-11ea-ba47-43a4e54bd116.html#:~:text=But%20that's%20not%20Johnso

n's%20style.&text=Johnson%20also%20set%20a%20new,90
%2Dhole%20Bob%20Hope%20Classic.

[33] Guinness World Records,
https://www.guinnessworldrecords.com/world-records/longest-golf-carry-at-altitude-below-1000-m

[34] Guinness Book of Records, Golf,
https://www.guinnessworldrecords.com/world-records/fastest-round-of-golf-fourball

[35] Guinness Book of Records, Golf,
https://www.guinnessworldrecords.com/search?term=golf